"Just what the doctor ordered"

HEALTH AND GROOMING

IN THE CLASSIC AGE OF ADVERTISING

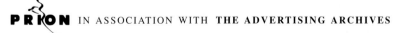

PRION IN ASSOCIATION WITH **THE ADVERTISING ARCHIVES**

First published in 1999
by Prion Books
An imprint of
Carlton Publishing
20 Mortimer Street
London W1T 3JW

Reprinted 2002, 2003, 2005

ISBN 1-85375-350-5

All images courtesy of The Advertising Archives, London
Many thanks to Suzanne, Alison and Emma
Cover design by Bob Eames
Printed and bound in China by Leo Paper Products Ltd

MAKES CHILDREN AND ADULTS AS FAT AS PIGS.

NO CURE NO PAY

Price 50 Cents.

GROVE'S TASTELESS CHILL TONIC

ON THE MARKET OVER 20 YEARS

1½ MILLION BOTTLES SOLD LAST YEAR

"JUST WHAT THE DOCTOR ORDERED" – HEALTH AND GROOMING IN THE CLASSIC AGE OF ADVERTISING

PRION BOOKS LTD Imperial Works, Perren Street, London NW5 3ED

"JUST WHAT THE DOCTOR ORDERED" – HEALTH AND GROOMING IN THE CLASSIC AGE OF ADVERTISING

PRION BOOKS LTD Imperial Works, Perren Street, London NW5 3ED

"JUST WHAT THE DOCTOR ORDERED" – HEALTH AND GROOMING IN THE CLASSIC AGE OF ADVERTISING
PRION BOOKS LTD Imperial Works, Perren Street, London NW5 3ED

"JUST WHAT THE DOCTOR ORDERED" – HEALTH AND GROOMING IN THE CLASSIC AGE OF ADVERTISING
PRION BOOKS LTD Imperial Works, Perren Street, London NW5 3ED

"JUST WHAT THE DOCTOR ORDERED" – HEALTH AND GROOMING IN THE CLASSIC AGE OF ADVERTISING
PRION BOOKS LTD Imperial Works, Perren Street, London NW5 3ED

Ashamed of Corns

As People Should Be—They Are So Unnecessary

The instinct is to hide a corn. And to cover the pain with a smile.

For people nowadays know that a corn is passé. And that naught but neglect can account for it.

It is like a torn gown which you fail to repair. Or a spot which you fail to remove. The fault lies in neglecting a few-minute duty—just as with a corn.

Any corn pain can be stopped in a moment, and stopped for good. Any corn can be ended quickly and completely.

All that is necessary is to apply a little Blue-jay plaster. It is done in a jiffy. It means no inconvenience.

Then a bit of scientific wax begins its gentle action. In two days, usually, the whole corn disappears. Some old, tough corns require a second application, but not often.

Can you think of a reason for paring corns and letting them continue? Or for using harsh or mussy applications? Or of clinging to any old-time method which is now taboo?

Or for suffering corns—for spoiling hours—when millions of others escape?

Can you think of a reason for not trying Blue-jay? It is a modern scientific treatment, invented by a famous chemist. It is made by a house of world-wide fame in the making of surgical dressings.

It has ended corns by the tens of millions—corns which are just like yours. It is easy and gentle and sure, as you can prove for yourself tonight.

Try Blue-jay on one corn. If it does as we say, keep it by you. On future corns apply it the moment they appear. That will mean perpetual freedom. A corn ache, after that, will be unknown to you.

BᴵB Blue=jay
For Corns

Stops Pain Instantly—Ends Corns Completely

Large Package 25c at Druggists
Small Package Discontinued
(888)

How Blue=jay Acts

A is a thin, soft pod which stops the pain by relieving the pressure.

B is the B&B wax, which gently undermines the corn. Usually it takes only 48 hours to end the corn completely.

C is rubber adhesive which sticks without wetting. It wraps around the toe and makes the plaster snug and comfortable.

Blue-jay is applied in a jiffy. After that, one doesn't feel the corn. The action is gentle, and applied to the corn alone. So the corn disappears without soreness.

BAUER & BLACK, *Makers of Surgical Dressings, etc.,* **CHICAGO and NEW YORK**

"JUST WHAT THE DOCTOR ORDERED" – HEALTH AND GROOMING IN THE CLASSIC AGE OF ADVERTISING
PRION BOOKS LTD Imperial Works, Perren Street, London NW5 3ED

—and he wonders why
she said "NO!"

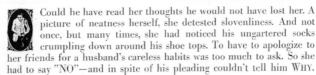

Could he have read her thoughts he would not have lost her. A picture of neatness herself, she detested slovenliness. And not once, but many times, she had noticed his ungartered socks crumpling down around his shoe tops. To have to apologize to her friends for a husband's careless habits was too much to ask. So she had to say "NO"—and in spite of his pleading couldn't tell him WHY.

No SOX Appeal Without

SINGLE GRIP

PARIS
GARTERS
NO METAL CAN TOUCH YOU
25c to 82
Dress Well and Succeed

DOUBLE GRIP

No Sox Appeal – "she detested slovenliness… to have to apologize to her friends for a husband's careless habits was too much to ask" (1928)

"JUST WHAT THE DOCTOR ORDERED" – HEALTH AND GROOMING IN THE CLASSIC AGE OF ADVERTISING

PRION BOOKS LTD Imperial Works, Perren Street, London NW5 3ED

Halitosis makes *you unpopular*

It is inexcusable . . . . . . can be instantly remedied.

NO matter how charming you may be or how fond of you your friends are, you cannot expect them to put up with halitosis (unpleasant breath) forever. They may be nice to you—but it is an effort.

Don't fool yourself that you never have halitosis as do so many self-assured people who constantly offend this way.

Read the facts in the lower right-hand corner and you will see that your chance of escape is slight. Nor should you count on being able to detect this ailment in yourself. Halitosis doesn't announce itself. You are seldom aware you have it.

Recognizing these truths, nice people end any chance of offending by systematically rinsing the mouth with Listerine. Every

morning. Every night. And between times when necessary, especially before meeting others.

Keep a bottle handy in home and office for this purpose.

Listerine ends halitosis instantly. Being antiseptic, it strikes at its commonest cause—fermentation in the oral cavity. Then, being a powerful deodorant, it destroys the odors themselves.

If you have any doubt of Listerine's powerful deodorant properties, make this test: Rub a slice of onion on your hand. Then apply Listerine clear. Immediately, every trace of onion odor is gone. Even the strong odor of fish yields to it. Lambert Pharmacal Company, St. Louis, Mo., U. S. A.

The new baby—
LISTERINE SHAVING CREAM
—you've got a treat ahead of you.
TRY IT

READ THE FACTS
⅓ had halitosis

68 hairdressers state that about every third woman, many of them from the wealthy classes, is halitosic. Who should know better than they?

LISTERINE
The safe antiseptic

"No matter how charming you may be or how fond of you your friends are, you cannot expect them to put up with halitosis forever" **(1928)**

"JUST WHAT THE DOCTOR ORDERED" – HEALTH AND GROOMING IN THE CLASSIC AGE OF ADVERTISING
PRION BOOKS LTD Imperial Works, Perren Street, London NW5 3ED

it disgusts—it repels—it's inexcusable!

get rid of that dandruff

You can get rid of that humiliating condition known as loose dandruff so easily by using Listerine. That is a strong statement. You expect us to back it up. We are content to rest our case on the product itself. Since it has helped tens of thousands of others, we expect it to help you.

Forget any troubles and failures you may have had as a result of using harsh antiseptics, and give Listerine a thorough trial.

Results achieved quickly

You simply use Listerine as a part of the shampoo, or independent of it. Douse it on the scalp full strength and massage vigorously. Keep the treatment up, using a little olive oil if the scalp is excessively dry. You will be delighted to see how quick-

ly you get results. Frequently loose dandruff disappears after one or two treatments. Sometimes, however, if the case is stubborn, a week or two and perhaps more will be required.

Infection makes fat glands overactive

Dandruff is caused by overactivity of the fat glands of the scalp— which expel a greasy, whitish substance known as sebum. This overactivity is the result of infection, many dermatologists claim. They advise immediate treatment. Whatever the cause, this activity should be checked lest the condition continue and cause eczema, falling hair, and baldness.

Why Listerine checks dandruff

Frequent shampoo, vigorous massage, and the use

of an antiseptic constitute effective treatment for ordinary cases of loose dandruff.

The success of Listerine in combating this condition is due to certain unusual qualities.

Since it is a safe though powerful germicide, Listerine combats any irritation that may be present on the scalp.

It dissolves and removes incrustations of sebum from the hair and scalp, assuring antiseptic cleanliness. It produces on the scalp an astringent effect, exhilarates and invigorates the tissue around the hair roots.

It allays itching, and soothes inflammation and eruption frequently associated with dandruff.

Send for our **FREE BOOKLET OF ETIQUETTE** — tells what to wear, say, and do at social affairs. Address, Dept. S.6, Lambert Pharmacal Company, St. Louis, Mo.

shampoo with Listerine
The Safe Antiseptic

"It disgusts, it repels, it's inexcusable – get rid of that dandruff"
(1929)

"JUST WHAT THE DOCTOR ORDERED" – HEALTH AND GROOMING IN THE CLASSIC AGE OF ADVERTISING
PRION BOOKS LTD Imperial Works, Perren Street, London NW5 3ED

He took his girl swimming and gave her
Athlete's Foot

HE WAS A ★
CARRIER

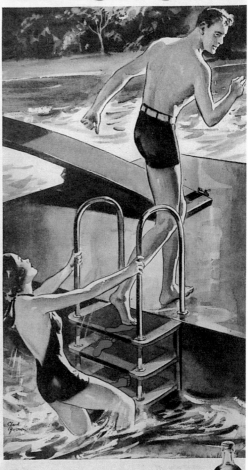

NO ONE is safe in the company of a victim of Athlete's Foot, when their bare feet tread the same surfaces.

For a single carrier of Athlete's Foot—a woman, child or man—may infect scores of other people who are so luckless as to follow in the bath house at the beach, in the shower or locker-room at the club, on the edge of a swimming pool, or even in the family bathroom.

Red skin is the mark of the Carrier

If you suspect you have a case of Athlete's Foot, you may be in danger as grave to yourself as to others who may contract it from you; use Absorbine Jr. promptly.

Don't take chances. Examine the skin between your toes. If it looks red, itches, stings or burns, you'll welcome the cooling, soothing relief brought by applications of Absorbine Jr. You may save yourself a lot of painful trouble.

For Athlete's Foot is caused by an insidious fungus that digs and bores deeper into the skin, when neglected—resulting in unwholesome whiteness and moistness, peeling skin, cracks and painful rawness.

Absorbine Jr. destroys the fungus

Even in advanced stages, Absorbine Jr. relieves the condition and helps to soothe and heal the damaged tissues. If, however, you feel your case is really serious, by all means consult your doctor in addition to the use of Absorbine Jr., morning and night.

When you buy, insist upon genuine Absorbine Jr. and accept no imitations offered as being "just as good." This famous remedy has been tested and proved for its ability to kill the fungus when reached, a fungus so stubborn that infected socks must be boiled 20 minutes to destroy it.

Absorbine Jr. is economical to use because it takes so little to bring relief. Also wonderful for the bites of insects, such as mosquitoes and jiggers. At all druggists, $1.25 a bottle. For free sample, write W. F. Young, Inc., 217 Lyman Street, Springfield, Massachusetts.

★ "Carrier" is the medical term for a person who carries infection. People infected with Athlete's Foot are "carriers." And at least one-half of all adults suffer from it (Athlete's Foot) at some time, according to the U. S. Public Health Service. They spread the disease wherever they tread barefoot.

ABSORBINE JR.
Relieves sore muscles, muscular aches, bruises, sprains and Sunburn

"JUST WHAT THE DOCTOR ORDERED" – HEALTH AND GROOMING IN THE CLASSIC AGE OF ADVERTISING

PRION BOOKS LTD Imperial Works, Perren Street, London NW5 3ED

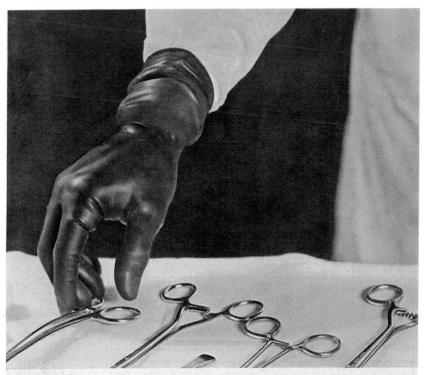

... often the only relief
from toilet tissue illness

THE annual reports issued by public hospitals show an astonishing percentage of rectal cases . . . many of which require surgical treatment.

Physicians who specialize in ailments of this kind estimate that 65 per cent of all men and women over 40 suffer from some form of rectal illness.

Many of these cases are directly traceable to inferior toilet tissue. Harsh, chemically impure toilet tissue—made from reclaimed waste material.

To be safe, millions of housewives and purchasing agents buying for schools, office buildings and industrial plants insist on the tissues that doctors and hospitals approve—ScotTissue

and Waldorf. These two health tissues are made from fresh new materials, specially processed to obtain an extremely soft, cloth-like texture. They are *twice as absorbent* as ordinary kinds.

Without this degree of absorbency, thorough hygiene is impossible.

You can rely on Scott Tissues to protect your family's health—just as doctors and hospitals rely on them to protect the health of their patients.

Eliminate a needless risk. Ask for ScotTissue or Waldorf when you order. They cost no more than inferior tissues. Scott Paper Company, Chester, Pa. In Canada, Scott Paper Co., Ltd., Toronto, Ont.

SCOTTISSUE, *an extremely soft, pure white, absorbent roll containing 1,000 sheets*

2 for 25¢
Price for U. S. only

WALDORF, *soft and absorbent, yet inexpensive. Any family can afford this fine tissue* **3 for 20¢**
Price for U. S. only

Doctors, Hospitals, Health Authorities approve **Scott Tissues** for Safety

"JUST WHAT THE DOCTOR ORDERED" – HEALTH AND GROOMING IN THE CLASSIC AGE OF ADVERTISING

Prion Books Ltd Imperial Works, Perren Street, London NW5 3ED

WHY I CRIED AFTER THE PARTY

One of the thousands of letters that come to the makers of Lifebuoy

" I KNEW I WAS THE BEST DANCER IN THE HALL. BUT AFTER THE FIRST FEW DANCES, THE MEN DRIFTED AWAY. LIKE EVERY PARTY IT ENDED IN TEARS FOR ME."

" A GIRL, THE TRUEST FRIEND IN THE WORLD, TOLD ME THE <u>REAL</u> REASON. I WAS HORRIFIED! COULD I OFFEND <u>THAT</u> WAY?"

" NEVER SINCE THAT DAY HAVE I BEEN WITHOUT MY STAUNCHEST ALLY — LIFEBUOY. IT ENDED 'B.O.'"

" LIFEBUOY HAS BEEN AN 'OPEN SESAME' INTO LIFE FOR ME. MY DANCE PROGRAM IS ALWAYS FULL. DO YOU WONDER I AM DEEPLY GRATEFUL?"

TRUE "B.O." EXPERIENCE NO. 321

This letter, in picture form, is from a young person who really suffered for her own carelessness . . . One of thousands of letters telling heartbreaking stories of broken romances, lost business opportunities, marriages that ended unhappily —all because the writers didn't make *sure*.

HOW DO YOU KEEP YOUR SKIN SO LOVELY?

I JUST NEVER USE ANYTHING BUT LIFEBUOY!

Don't cry about your complexion! If it's dull, tired, Lifebuoy will revive it, help renew its loveliness! It cleanses more deeply, yet *gently* . . . "Patch" tests on the skins of hundreds of women show Lifebuoy is more than 20% milder than many so-called "beauty soaps."

Take this warning to heart!

Follow this simple rule, and you'll never need to worry about offending: Bathe regularly with Lifebuoy. Let its creamy, deep-searching lather keep you *fresh!* Lathers abundantly, even in hardest water. Purifies pores, stops "B.O." *(body odor)*. Its own clean scent rinses away.

Approved by Good Housekeeping Bureau

ITS 52% "MOISTER" LATHER SOAKS WHISKERS SOFT

JACK, YOU ALWAYS WERE SO NEAT BEFORE WE WERE MARRIED. NOW YOU'RE EVEN CARELESS ABOUT SHAVING

NOT CARELESS, DEAR. SHAVING EVERY DAY GETS MY TENDER SKIN SO RAW, I HAVE TO REST MY FACE NOW AND THEN

MY BROTHER BILL HAD THAT TROUBLE, TOO. HE CHANGED TO LIFEBUOY SHAVING CREAM. NOW HIS FACE IS NEVER SORE. HE SAYS THAT'S BECAUSE LIFEBUOY LATHER IS LOTS MILDER

THAT SO? I'LL TRY THAT, YOU BET! MUST GET A TUBE RIGHT AWAY

AT LAST! A LATHER THAT REALLY STAYS MOIST, SOFTENS MY STIFF BEARD SO I CAN'T FEEL IT COMING OFF! AND IT'S SOOTHING, TOO

Send for a FREE Trial Tube

Lifebuoy Shaving Cream's ability to soak up 52% more moisture assures a softer beard—an easier shave. Try it. Get the big red tube at your druggist's. Or write Lever Brothers Co., Dept. A163, Cambridge, Mass., for a free 12-day trial tube.

(This offer good in U. S. only)

120 TO 150 SHAVES IN THE BIG FULL-SIZED TUBE

"JUST WHAT THE DOCTOR ORDERED" – HEALTH AND GROOMING IN THE CLASSIC AGE OF ADVERTISING
PRION BOOKS LTD Imperial Works, Perren Street, London NW5 3ED

"Mary was so fidgety she couldn't concentrate...

...I was shocked to find that harsh toilet tissue was the cause"

"JUST WHAT THE DOCTOR ORDERED" – HEALTH AND GROOMING IN THE CLASSIC AGE OF ADVERTISING
PRION BOOKS LTD Imperial Works, Perren Street, London NW5 3ED

"*You've certainly* stopped *Sneaker Smell*"

"*Phew! I knew that smell was Ted's sneakers*"

NO MORE OF THIS

declare Parents all over the Country

The family war on sneakers is over! No more complaints about excessive perspiration odor from fathers and mothers.

For Hood Canvas Shoes — with the Hygeen Insole perfected by Hood chemists — absolutely prevent that offensive perspiration odor which ordinary sneakers develop! No wonder we are getting enthusiastic reports from parents all over the entire country.

How does it work? Ordinary sneakers get smelly because they soak up perspiration. But the Hygeen Insole *cannot* soak up perspiration. It is non-absorbent. Therefore, the moisture *evaporates* quickly from Hood Canvas Shoes!

Here are the ideal shoes for hot weather. Cool, comfortable, sanitary. Here are the canvas shoes that children like and parents need no longer worry about. Inexpensive, too, in spite of their extra feature — the Hygeen Insole. Avoid offensive "sneaker smell" this season! Get Hood Canvas Shoes at your local store.

Adv. Copyright Hood Rubber Co., Inc., 1933

3 IMPORTANT POINTS ON HOOD CANVAS SHOES

1. VENTILATED: Tiny air spaces let fresh air shoot right *through* the canvas uppers, keeping youngsters' feet cool and comfortable.

2. WASHABLE: No artificial stiffening to wash out and leave the canvas limp. Use ordinary soap and water and they'll be fresh and firm as new!

3. XTRULOCK PROCESS: By this patented *process* many Hood models (including shoe illustrated) are molded together into one complete unit. No stitches to break — no seams to chafe feet and wear out socks.

Patent applied for

Look inside the shoe for this mark

Hygeen Insole

on the Green Insole for your protection

HOOD CANVAS SHOES

Hood Rubber Company, Inc., Watertown, Mass.

Reduce Unemployment **BUY AMERICAN** Made Merchandise

"JUST WHAT THE DOCTOR ORDERED" – HEALTH AND GROOMING IN THE CLASSIC AGE OF ADVERTISING
PRION BOOKS LTD Imperial Works, Perren Street, London NW5 3ED

"AND JONES, DON'T FORGET—THIS JOB CALLS FOR _PLEASING PERSONALITY_"

Grouches—bad temper—are often signs of a run-down physical condition

PERSONALITY has a lot to do with holding down a job. If you're edgy . . . depressed mentally . . . and go around with a chip on your shoulder, you can't expect to make a good impression.

Often, people are called difficult to get along with—when the truth is they are overtired, physically run-down.

The cause is usually an "underfed" condition of the blood. Your blood feeds your body. When it is "underfed," there's not enough nourishment carried to your nerves and muscles to keep your energy up to par. As a result you become low-spirited and generally out of sorts.

How a Simple Food Stabilizes the Nerves

Fleischmann's fresh Yeast increases the activity of the digestive organs—and helps to put more food into the blood stream. In this way more nourishment is carried to the muscle and nerve tissues throughout the body. Your whole system responds with new energy. You soon regain your poise—feel like a new person.

Eat 3 cakes of Fleischmann's Yeast regularly each day—before meals. Eat it plain, or on crackers—or dissolved in a little water or fruit juice. Start today—see how quickly depression and that "tired feeling" disappear.

GENIAL AND FRIENDLY in _all_ your relationships —that's your normal state when you're glowing with health. But when your energy gets below par, it's difficult to do your work and keep pleasant. Keep well— then it's easy to keep cheerful and popular.

It's your blood that "FEEDS" your body

ONE of the important functions of your blood stream is to carry nourishment from your food to the muscle and nerve tissues of your entire body.

When you feel "overtired" at the least little extra effort, it is usually a sign that your blood is not supplied with enough food for your tissues.

What you need is something to provide the full nourishment from your food, so that there is more food for your blood to take up and carry to your tissues.

"IT WAS A SERIOUS MATTER WITH ME when I lost my energy. I worried when I realized I was no longer as alert as I should be. I was tired before the day began—could hardly drag myself out of bed. I let everything slip along. I was irritable. That doesn't get you very far.

"Then I took Fleischmann's Yeast. In two or three days the inertia disappeared. You ought to see me in the morning now. After a good sleep I can tear off hours of work without a stop. Fleischmann's Yeast is really important in my life, and I'd hate to have to be without it."

Rhodes A. Patterson, Ruston, La.

corrects Run-down condition
by feeding and purifying the blood

"Personality has a lot to do with holding down a job. If you're edgy… depressed mentally…and go around with a chip on your shoulder, you can't expect to make a good impression" (1936)

"JUST WHAT THE DOCTOR ORDERED" – HEALTH AND GROOMING IN THE CLASSIC AGE OF ADVERTISING

PRION BOOKS LTD Imperial Works, Perren Street, London NW5 3ED

A BED TIME SUCCESS STORY

LORD PEPPERELL
SANFORIZED-SHRUNK
Pajamas
TAILORED by WELDON

You're hearing about pajamas in which you can woo Morpheus with *smartness* and *comfort*. Sanforized-Shrunk puts an honest-to-goodness "No Shrinking" sign on these handsome Lord Pepperell pajamas. Perfect fit doesn't pass out of the picture with a visit or two to the laundry. No more up-crawling sleeves and trouser legs. No more body constriction to ruin good sleeping. Instead, the lasting satisfaction of garments that do not shrink out of fit. Stock up some of these Lord Pepperells without delay. 12 exclusive patterns. Coats (and pants) of many colors. Tailoring of the high order for which Weldon is celebrated. Get lasting satisfaction at 2.00 per pair. If dealer cannot supply you, write to

LUBIN-WEEKER CO., INC., (Makers of Weldon), 1270 Broadway, New York City.

Lord Pepperell
DE LUXE

A particular group of de luxe styles in 8 solid colors. Tailored with the Weldon touch. All fabrics Sanforized-Shrunk. Price 2.50.

Sanforized-Shrunk
40 WORTH STREET   NEW YORK CITY

"JUST WHAT THE DOCTOR ORDERED" – HEALTH AND GROOMING IN THE CLASSIC AGE OF ADVERTISING
PRION BOOKS LTD Imperial Works, Perren Street, London NW5 3ED

"JUST WHAT THE DOCTOR ORDERED" – HEALTH AND GROOMING IN THE CLASSIC AGE OF ADVERTISING

PRION BOOKS LTD Imperial Works, Perren Street, London NW5 3ED

Why not get a *Lovely Figure* for Spring

IF you want to dress inexpensively, and be able to wear standard fittings with charm and distinction, start now to get rid of that accumulated Winter fat. With the help of nightly Bile Beans you can 'slim while you sleep' safely and gradually.

Bile Beans are purely vegetable. Besides dispersing unwanted fat and ensuring regular daily elimination, Bile Beans purify and enrich your blood, clear your skin and improve health and vitality.

So to be attractively slim and for radiant health, take Bile Beans regularly each night.

Healthier Without Excess Fat

"Soon after starting to take nightly Bile Beans I found they were not only improving my health, but surely removing the unwanted fat. Since then I have lost something like 28 pounds and as a result feel fitter and healthier in every way."—Mrs. M. H., Harrow.

Can Wear Standard Dresses

"Bile Beans have made my figure so much slimmer that now standard dresses and coats fit me perfectly. Bile Beans have also given me a lovely clear skin, and made me feel ever so fit."—Miss A. D., Cheshire.

SOLD EVERYWHERE

BILE BEANS
Make You Slim and Keep You Fit

"JUST WHAT THE DOCTOR ORDERED" – HEALTH AND GROOMING IN THE CLASSIC AGE OF ADVERTISING

PRION BOOKS LTD Imperial Works, Perren Street, London NW5 3ED

Family doctors, surgeons, diagnos-ticians, nose and throat specialists ... doctors in every branch of medicine were asked: "What cigarette do you smoke, Doctor?"

Three nationally known independent research organizations did the asking.

The answers came in by the thousands. Actual state-ments from doctors themselves. Figures were checked and re-checked! The results? Camels ... convincingly!

R. J. Reynolds Tobacco Co., Winston-Salem, North Carolina

According to this recent Nationwide survey:

MORE DOCTORS SMOKE CAMELS THAN ANY OTHER CIGARETTE!

This is no casual claim. It's an actual fact. Based on the statements of doctors themselves to three nationally known independent research organizations.

THE QUESTION was very simple. One that you...any smoker ... might ask a doctor: "What cigarette do you smoke, Doctor?"

After all, doctors are human too. Like you, they smoke for pleasure. Their taste, like yours, enjoys the pleasing flavor of costlier tobaccos. Their throats too appreciate a cool mildness.

And more doctors named Camels than any other cigarette!

If you are a Camel smoker, this preference for Camels among physicians and surgeons will not surprise you. But if you are not now smoking Camels, by all means try them. Compare them critically in your "T-Zone" (see right).

CAMEL—COSTLIER TOBACCOS

THE "T-ZONE" TEST WILL TELL YOU

The "T-Zone"—T for taste and T for throat—is your own proving ground for any cigarette. Only your taste and throat can decide which cigarette tastes best to you ... how it affects your throat. On the basis of the experience of many, many millions of smok-ers, we believe Camels will suit your "T-Zone" to a "T."

"JUST WHAT THE DOCTOR ORDERED" – HEALTH AND GROOMING IN THE CLASSIC AGE OF ADVERTISING

PRION BOOKS LTD Imperial Works, Perren Street, London NW5 3ED

To Wake Up GAY in the Morning!

Just Try this at Bedtime Tonight!

Why be content to waken tired, listless, or low in the morning—when you should be gay and radiantly "alive"? Why not follow this simple plan thousands are using for sparkling morning freshness? Just drink a warm cup of Ovaltine at bedtime each night.

For here's what Ovaltine does to bring you fresher, happier mornings—

First, taken warm at bedtime, it promotes sound sleep, without drugs.

Second, it supplies specially processed food to rebuild vitality *while you sleep.*

Third, it also furnishes extra amounts of vitamins and minerals in a delicious, *more natural* way for all-round health and vigor.

So why not turn to Ovaltine tonight? See if you don't sleep better, feel more vital—if your friends don't tell you how much more radiant you look!

OVALTINE

PLAIN AND CHOCOLATE FLAVORED

"JUST WHAT THE DOCTOR ORDERED" – HEALTH AND GROOMING IN THE CLASSIC AGE OF ADVERTISING

PRION BOOKS LTD Imperial Works, Perren Street, London NW5 3ED

Don't let them whisper behind _your_ back!

Lifebuoy Health Soap is the _only_ soap especially made to stop "B.O." _(body odor)_ Remember, LIFEBUOY CONTAINS AN EXCLUSIVE PURIFYING INGREDIENT. A daily Lifebuoy bath gives you such _lasting_ all-over protection! And Lifebuoy is amazingly mild and refreshing. You'll be delighted with your exhilarating LIFEBUOY bath. Use Lifebuoy for a week and you'll use it _for life!_

Used in the homes of 40 million Americans.

The _refreshing_ bath
that gives lasting protection!
The Soap of Considerate People
use it daily

"JUST WHAT THE DOCTOR ORDERED" – HEALTH AND GROOMING IN THE CLASSIC AGE OF ADVERTISING
PRION BOOKS LTD Imperial Works, Perren Street, London NW5 3ED

6 A.M. . . . you're feeling punk

OH WOE! You wake up feeling punk because you need a laxative. What's to do about it? Get relief now—*when* *you need it*—speedy relief—easy relief! Take a glass of sparkling Sal Hepatica the minute you get up.

8 A.M. . . . you're full of spunk!

LET'S GO! You're feeling lots better already. Taken first thing in the morning, Sal Hepatica usually acts *within an hour* . . . brings fast yet gentle relief. In addition, it helps turn a sour stomach sweet again by helping counteract excess gastric acidity.

Remember . . . 3 out of 5 doctors, interviewed in a survey, recommend this sparkling saline laxative.

Remember Sal Hepatica when next *you* need a laxative.

SAL HEPATICA

"JUST WHAT THE DOCTOR ORDERED" – HEALTH AND GROOMING IN THE CLASSIC AGE OF ADVERTISING
PRION BOOKS LTD Imperial Works, Perren Street, London NW5 3ED

"JUST WHAT THE DOCTOR ORDERED" – HEALTH AND GROOMING IN THE CLASSIC AGE OF ADVERTISING
Prion Books Ltd Imperial Works, Perren Street, London NW5 3ED